SOLITARY
ANIMALS

SOLITARY ANIMALS

INTROVERTS OF THE WILD

by **Joshua David Stein**

art by **Dominique Ramsey**

RISE
NEW YORK

RISE × Penguin Workshop

An Imprint of Penguin Random House LLC, New York

Visit us online at www.penguinrandomhouse.com.

The text is set in Good Headline Pro.
The art was created using an Apple iPad, Procreate, and Photoshop.

Edited by Cecily Kaiser
Designed by Maria Elias

Library of Congress Control Number: 2021013780

ISBN 9780593384435   Special Markets ISBN: 9780593661086 Not for resale   10 9 8 7 6 5 4 3 2 1   RRD-Asia

This Imagination Library edition is published by Penguin Young Readers, a division of Penguin Random House, exclusively for Dolly Parton's Imagination Library, a not-for-profit program designed to inspire a love of reading and learning, sponsored in part by The Dollywood Foundation. Penguin's trade editions of this work are available wherever books are sold.

At the watering hole,

a parade of elephants pass by.

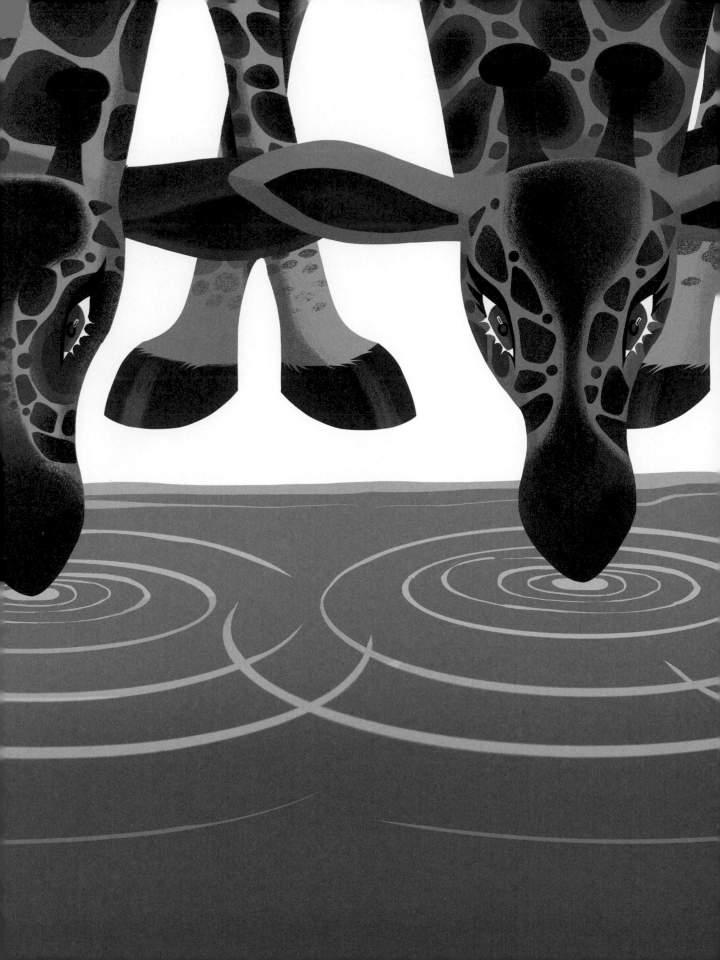

A tower of giraffes bend their long necks down for a drink . . .

And a dazzle
of zebras, brilliant,
brown and white,
blink in the hot sun.

But the panther arrives
by herself.

The panther is a
solitary animal.

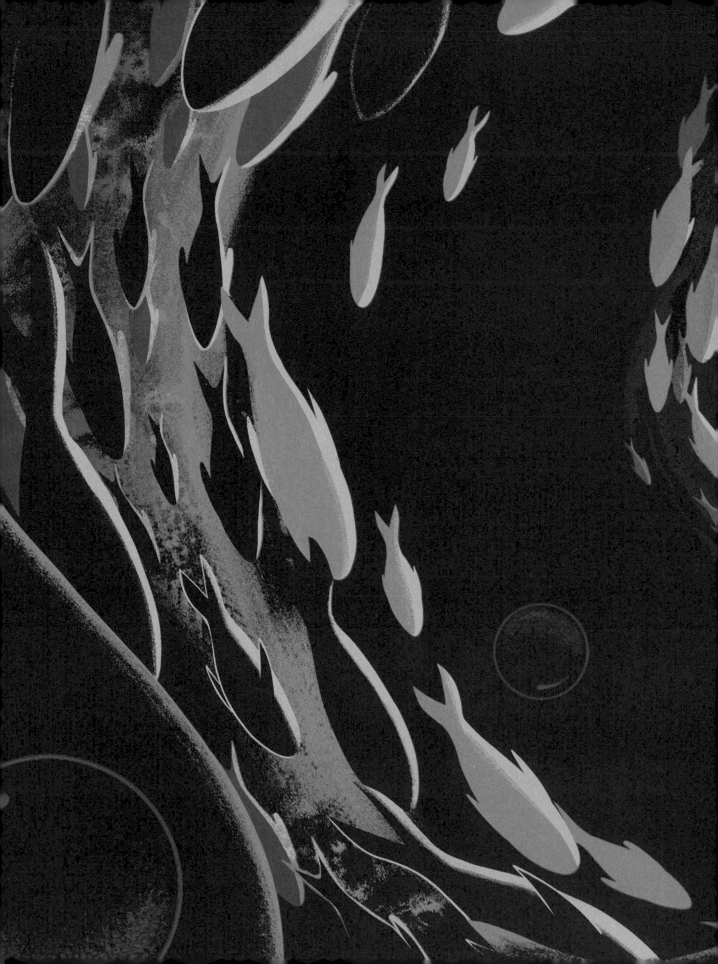

That silvery cloud
swimming in the sea is
actually a school of fish.

That splash and crash is
a pod of whales sounding.

Behold, a fever of stingrays
gliding by.

But what do you call
a group of octopuses?

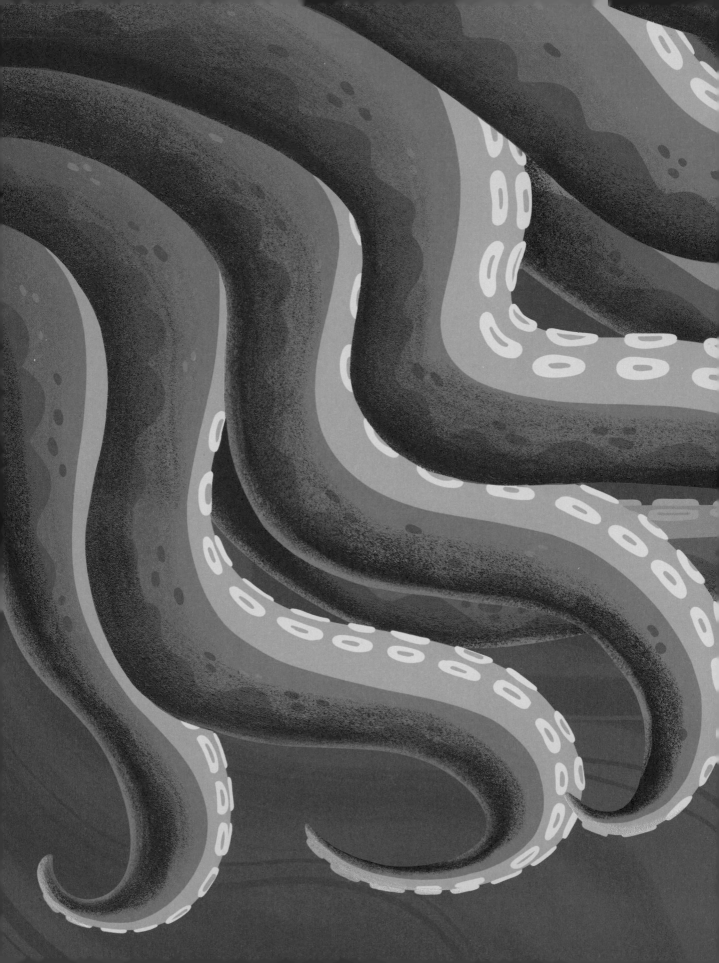

A tangle of octopuses?

A chandelier of octopuses?

A *multipus* of octopuses?

No, octopuses
prefer to be alone.

The octopus is a
solitary animal.

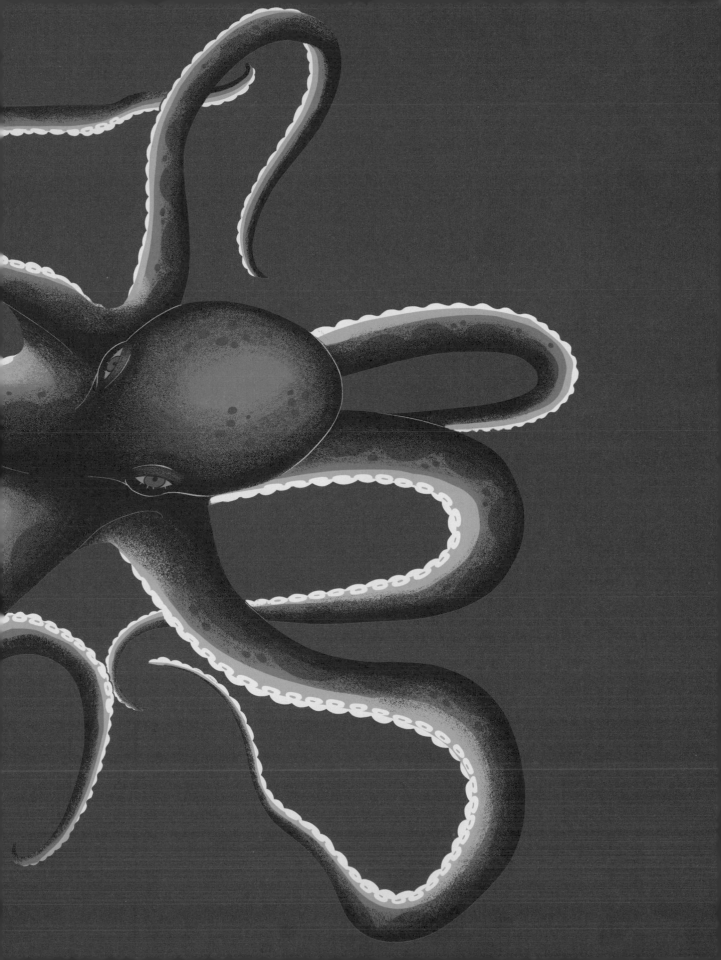

The sloth is . . .

. . . a solitary . . .

. . . animal, too.

A swarm of swallows
is called a gulp.

A huddle of
hummingbirds
is a charm.

Pigeons,

flying together,

are called a kit.

But what do you call
a group of eagles?
Nothing at all.

An eagle is a
solitary animal.

From the ground,

she looks like a lonely speck.

But from up in the sky,
the eagle sees all the
world below.

She sees not just dazzles, fevers,
and gulps, but a sloth smiling slowly,
and a panther stalking silently,
and an octopus dancing by himself.

They may appear alone like her,
but they aren't. Not really.
For there's a whole world of
solitary animals out there.

Alone.

Together.

Happy.

MORE ABOUT
SOLITARY ANIMALS

Why are some animals solitary and others not?

It is a matter of survival. Some animals have evolved to survive alone. Other animals, called social animals, have evolved to survive better in a group. It depends on many things such as the size of the animal, how many babies they have, and whether there's enough food to feed a group of animals together or just one.

Are solitary animals taught to be solitary?

A solitary animal is solitary by instinct, which means they don't need to be taught to be alone. They simply prefer it that way. It is very important that every animal, solitary or not, learns to listen to their feelings, or instincts, which help them figure out the best way to live and survive.

Are solitary animals always solitary or do they sometimes live with others?

Solitary animals are often, but not always, alone. They come together to mate, sometimes to hunt, and sometimes to ask for help from other animals. A vampire bat, for instance, is a solitary animal but if it is hungry, it sometimes asks other bats for a bite to eat.

Do solitary animals miss their mommies and daddies?

No. After some time, which can range from almost none for octopuses to two years for alligators, a solitary animal has developed the skills to be self-reliant, which means they have learned to feed themselves and defend themselves. It is the job of their parents to help them learn those skills. But after that, the animals are happy to be alone, even from their mommies and daddies.

Are humans solitary animals?

Not really. Humans are social animals who sometimes prefer or need to be alone. In fact, social animals are not social all the time, and solitary animals are not solitary all the time, either. All creatures find their own balance.